The Raven

by
Edgar Allan Poe

Illustrated by
Gustave Doré

COMMENT ON THE POEM

The secret of a poem, no less than a jest's prosperity, lies in the ear of him that hears it. Yield to its spell, accept the poet's mood: this, after all, is what the sages answer when you ask them of its value. Even though the poet himself, in his other mood, tell you that his art is but sleight of hand, his food enchanter's food, and offer to show you the trick of it,—believe him not. Wait for his prophetic hour; then give yourself to his passion, his joy or pain. "We are in Love's hand to-day!" sings Gautier, in Swinburne's buoyant paraphrase,—and from morn to sunset we are wafted on the violent sea: there is but one love, one May, one flowery strand. Love is eternal, all else unreal and put aside. The vision has an end, the scene changes; but we have gained something, the memory of a charm. As many poets, so many charms. There is the charm of Evanescence, that which lends to supreme beauty and grace an aureole of Pathos. Share with Landor his one "night of memories and of sighs" for Rose Aylmer, and you have this to the full.

And now take the hand of a new-world minstrel, strayed from some proper habitat to that rude and dissonant America which, as Baudelaire saw, "was for Poe only a vast prison through which he ran, hither and thither, with the feverish agitation of a being created to breathe in a purer world," and where "his interior life, spiritual as a poet, spiritual even as a drunkard, was but one perpetual effort to escape the influence of this antipathetical atmosphere." Clasp the sensitive hand of a troubled singer dreeing thus his weird, and share with him the clime in which he found,—never throughout the day, always in the night,—if not the Atlantis whence he had wandered, at least a place of refuge from the bounds in which by day he was immured.

To one land only he has power to lead you, and for one night only can you share his dream. A tract of neither Earth nor Heaven: "No-man's-land," out of Space, out of Time. Here are the perturbed ones, through whose eyes, like those of the Cenci, the soul finds windows though the mind is dazed; here spirits, groping for the path which leads to Eternity, are halted and delayed. It is the limbo of "planetary souls," wherein are all moonlight uncertainties, all lost loves and illusions. Here some are fixed in trance, the only respite attainable; others

> "move fantastically
> To a discordant melody:"

while everywhere are

> "Sheeted Memories of the Past—
> Shrouded forms that start and sigh
> As they pass the wanderer by."

Such is the land, and for one night we enter it,—a night of astral phases and recurrent chimes. Its monodies are twelve poems, whose music strives to change yet ever is the same. One by one they sound, like the chiming of the brazen and ebony clock, in "The Masque of the Red

Death," which made the waltzers pause with "disconcert and tremulousness and meditation," as often as the hour came round.

Of all these mystical cadences, the plaint of *The Raven*, vibrating through the portal, chiefly has impressed the outer world. What things go to the making of a poem,—and how true in this, as in most else, that race which named its bards "the makers"? A work is called out of the void. Where there was nothing, it remains,—a new creation, part of the treasure of mankind. And a few exceptional lyrics, more than others that are equally creative, compel us to think anew how bravely the poet's pen turns things unknown

> "to shapes, and gives to airy nothing
> A local habitation, and a name."

Each seems without a prototype, yet all fascinate us with elements wrested from the shadow of the Supernatural. Now the highest imagination is concerned about the soul of things; it may or may not inspire the Fantasy that peoples with images the interlunar vague. Still, one of these lyrics, in its smaller way, affects us with a sense of uniqueness, as surely as the sublimer works of a supernatural cast,— Marlowe's "Faustus," the "Faust" of Goethe, "Manfred," or even those ethereal masterpieces, "The Tempest" and "A Midsummer Night's Dream." More than one, while otherwise unique, has some burden or refrain which haunts the memory,—once heard, never forgotten, like the tone of a rarely used but distinctive organ-stop. Notable among them is Bürger's "Lenore," that ghostly and resonant ballad, the lure and foil of the translators. Few will deny that Coleridge's wondrous "Rime of the Ancient Mariner" stands at their very head. "Le Juif-Errant" would have claims, had Beranger been a greater poet; and, but for their remoteness from popular sympathy, "The Lady of Shalott" and "The Blessed Damozel" might be added to the list. It was given to Edgar Allan Poe to produce two lyrics, "The Bells" and *The Raven*, each of which, although perhaps of less beauty than those of Tennyson and Rossetti, is a unique. "Ulalume," while equally strange and imaginative, has not the universal quality that is a portion of our test.

The Raven in sheer poetical constituents falls below such pieces as "The Haunted Palace," "The City in the Sea," "The Sleeper," and "Israfel." The whole of it would be exchanged, I suspect, by readers of a fastidious cast, for such passages as these:

> "Around, by lifting winds forgot,
> Resignedly beneath the sky
> The melancholy waters lie.
> No rays from the holy heaven come down
> On the long night-time of that town;
> But light from out the lurid sea
> Streams up the turrets silently—
> . . . .
> Up many and many a marvellous shrine
> Whose wreathéd friezes intertwine
> The viol, the violet, and the vine.
> . . . .
> No swellings tell that winds may be
> Upon some far-off happier sea—
> No heavings hint that winds have been
> On seas less hideously serene."

It lacks the aerial melody of the poet whose heart-strings are a lute:

> "And they say (the starry choir
> And the other listening things)
> That Israfeli's fire
> Is owing to that lyre
> By which he sits and sings—
> The trembling living wire
> Of those unusual strings."

But *The Raven*, like "The Bells" and "Annabel Lee," commends itself to the many and the few. I have said elsewhere that Poe's rarer productions seemed to me "those in which there is the appearance, at least, of spontaneity,—in which he yields to his feelings, while dying falls and cadences most musical, most melancholy, come from him unawares."

This is still my belief; and yet, upon a fresh study of this poem, it impresses me more than at any time since my boyhood. Close acquaintance tells in favor of every true work of art. Induce the man, who neither knows art nor cares for it, to examine some poem or painting, and how soon its force takes hold of him! In fact, he will overrate the relative value of the first good work by which his attention has been fairly caught. *The Raven*, also, has consistent qualities which even an expert must admire. In no other of its author's poems is the motive more palpably defined. "The Haunted Palace" is just as definite to the select reader, but Poe scarcely would have taken that subtle allegory for bald analysis. *The Raven* is wholly occupied with the author's typical theme—the irretrievable loss of an idolized and beautiful woman; but on other grounds, also, the public instinct is correct in thinking it his representative poem.

A man of genius usually gains a footing with the success of some one effort, and this is not always his greatest. Recognition is the more instant for having been postponed. He does not acquire it, like a miser's fortune, coin after coin, but "not at all or all in all." And thus with other ambitions: the courtier, soldier, actor,—whatever their parts,—each counts his triumph from some lucky stroke. Poe's Raven, despite augury, was for him "the bird that made the breeze to blow." The poet settled in New-York, in the winter of 1844-'45, finding work upon Willis's paper, "The Evening Mirror," and eking out his income by contributions elsewhere. For six years he had been an active writer, and enjoyed a professional reputation; was held in both respect and misdoubt, and was at no loss for his share of the ill-paid journalism of that day. He also had done much of his very best work,—such tales as "Ligeia" and "The Fall of the House of Usher," (the latter containing that mystical counterpart, in verse, of Elihu Vedder's "A Lost Mind,") such analytic feats as "The Gold Bug" and "The Mystery of Marie Roget." He had made proselytes abroad, and gained a lasting hold upon the French mind. He had learned his own power and weakness, and was at his prime, and not without a certain reputation. But he had written nothing that was on the tongue of everybody. To rare and delicate work some popular touch must be added to capture the general audience of one's own time.

Through the industry of Poe's successive biographers, the hit made by *The Raven* has become an oft-told tale. The poet's young wife, Virginia, was fading before his eyes, but lingered for another year within death's shadow. The long, low chamber in the house near the Bloomingdale Road is as famous as the room where Rouget de l'Isle composed the Marseillaise. All have heard that the poem, signed "Quarles," appeared in the "American Review," with a pseudo-editorial comment on its form; that Poe received ten dollars for it; that Willis, the kindest and least envious of fashionable arbiters, reprinted it with a eulogy that instantly made it town-talk. All doubt of its authorship was dispelled when Poe recited it himself at a literary gathering, and for a time he was the most marked of American authors. The hit stimulated and encouraged him. Like another and prouder satirist, he too found "something of summer" even "in the hum of insects." Sorrowfully enough, but three years elapsed,—a period of influence, pride, anguish, yet always of imaginative or critical labor,—before the final defeat, before the curtain dropped on a life that for him was in truth a tragedy, and he yielded to "the Conqueror Worm."

"The American Review: A Whig Journal" was a creditable magazine for the time, double-columned, printed on good paper with clear type, and illustrated by mezzotint portraits. Amid much matter below the present standard, it contained some that any editor would be glad to receive. The initial volume, for 1845, has articles by Horace Greeley, Donald Mitchell, Walter Whitman, Marsh, Tuckerman, and Whipple. Ralph Hoyt's quaint poem, "Old," appeared in this volume. And here are three lyrics by Poe: "The City in the Sea," "The Valley of Unrest," and *The Raven*. Two of these were built up,—such was his way,—from earlier studies, but the last-named came out as if freshly composed, and almost as we have it now. The statement that it was not afterward revised is erroneous. Eleven trifling changes from the magazine-text appear in *The Raven and Other Poems*, 1845, a book which the poet shortly felt encouraged to offer the public. These are mostly changes of punctuation, or of single words, the latter kind made to heighten the effect of alliteration. In Mr. Lang's pretty edition of Poe's verse, brought out in the "Parchment Library," he has shown the instinct of a scholar, and has done wisely, in going back to the text in the volume just mentioned, as given in the London issue of 1846. The "standard" Griswold collection of the poet's works abounds with errors. These have been repeated by later editors, who also have made errors of their own. But the text of *The Raven*, owing to the requests made to the author for manuscript copies, was still farther revised by him; in fact, he printed it in Richmond, just before his death, with the poetic substitution of "seraphim whose foot-falls" for "angels whose faint foot-falls," in the fourteenth stanza. Our present text, therefore, while substantially that of 1845, is somewhat modified by the poet's later reading, and is, I think, the most correct and effective version of this single poem. The most radical change from the earliest version appeared, however, in the volume in 1845; the eleventh stanza originally having contained these lines, faulty in rhyme and otherwise a blemish on the poem:

"Caught from some unhappy master, whom unmerciful Disaster
Followed fast and followed faster—so, when Hope he would adjure,
Stern Despair returned, instead of the sweet Hope he dared adjure—
That sad answer, 'Nevermore!'"

It would be well if other, and famous, poets could be as sure of making their changes always improvements. Poe constantly rehandled his scanty show of verse, and usually bettered it. *The Raven* was the first of the few poems which he nearly brought to completion before printing. It may be that those who care for poetry lost little by his death. Fluent in prose, he never wrote verse for the sake of making a poem. When a refrain of image haunted him, the lyric that resulted was the inspiration, as he himself said, of a passion, not of a purpose. This was at intervals so rare as almost to justify the Fairfield theory that each was the product of a nervous crisis.

What, then, gave the poet his clue to *The Raven*? From what misty foundation did it rise slowly to a music slowly breathed? As usual, more than one thing went to the building of so notable a poem. Considering the longer sermons often preached on brief and less suggestive texts, I hope not to be blamed for this discussion of a single lyric,—especially one which an artist like Doré has made the subject of prodigal illustration. Until recently I had supposed that this piece, and a few which its author composed after its appearance, were exceptional in not having grown from germs in his boyish verse. But Mr. Fearing Gill has shown me some unpublished stanzas by Poe, written in his eighteenth year, and entitled, "The Demon of the Fire." The manuscript appears to be in the poet's early handwriting, and its genuineness is vouched for by the family in whose possession it has remained for half a century. Besides the plainest germs of "The Bells" and "The Haunted Palace" it contains a few lines somewhat suggestive of the opening and close of *The Raven.* As to the rhythm of our poem, a comparison of dates indicates that this was influenced by the rhythm of "Lady Geraldine's Courtship." Poe was one of the first to honor Miss Barrett's genius; he inscribed his collected poems to her as "the noblest of her sex," and was in sympathy with her lyrical method. The lines from her love-poem,

"With a murmurous stir uncertain, in the air, the purple curtain
Swelleth in and swelleth out around her motionless pale brows,"

found an echo in these:

"And the silken sad uncertain rustling of each purple curtain
Thrilled me—filled me with fantastic terrors never felt before."

Here Poe assumed a privilege for which he roughly censured Longfellow, and which no one ever sought on his own premises without swift detection and chastisement. In melody and stanzaic form, we shall see that the two poems are not unlike, but in motive they are totally distinct. The generous poetess felt nothing but the true originality of the poet. "This vivid writing!" she exclaimed,—"this power which is felt!... Our great poet, Mr. Browning, author of 'Paracelsus,' &c., is enthusiastic in his admiration of the rhythm." Mr. Ingram, after referring to "Lady Geraldine," cleverly points out another source from which Poe may have caught an impulse. In 1843, Albert Pike, the half-Greek, half-frontiersman, poet of Arkansas, had printed in "The New Mirror," for which Poe then was writing, some verses entitled "Isadore," but since revised by the author and called "The Widowed Heart." I select from Mr. Pike's revision the following stanza, of which the main features correspond with the original version:

"Restless I pace our lonely rooms, I play our songs no more,
The garish sun shines flauntingly upon the unswept floor;
The mocking-bird still sits and sings, O melancholy strain!
For my heart is like an autumn-cloud that overflows with rain;
Thou art lost to me forever, Isadore!"

Here we have a prolonged measure, a similarity of refrain, and the introduction of a bird whose song enhances sorrow. There are other trails which may be followed by the curious; notably, a passage which Mr. Ingram selects from Poe's final review of "Barnaby Rudge":

"The raven, too, * * * might have been made, more than we now see it, a portion of the conception of the fantastic Barnaby. * * * Its character might have performed, in regard to that of the idiot, much the same part as does, in music, the accompaniment in respect to the air."

Nevertheless, after pointing out these germs and resemblances, the value of this poem still is found in its originality. The progressive music, the scenic detail and contrasted light and shade,—above all, the spiritual passion of the nocturn, make it the work of an informing genius. As for the gruesome bird, he is unlike all the other ravens of his clan, from the "twa corbies" and "three ravens" of the balladists to Barnaby's rumpled "Grip." Here is no semblance of the cawing rook that haunts ancestral turrets and treads the field of heraldry; no boding phantom of which Tickell sang that, when,

"shrieking at her window thrice,
The raven flap'd his wing,
Too well the love-lorn maiden knew
The solemn boding sound."

Poe's raven is a distinct conception; the incarnation of a mourner's agony and hopelessness; a sable embodied Memory, the abiding chronicler of doom, a type of the Irreparable. Escaped across the Styx, from "the Night's Plutonian shore," he seems the imaged soul of the questioner himself,—of him who can not, will not, quaff the kind nepenthe, because the memory of Lenore is all that is left him, and with the surcease of his sorrow even that would be put aside.

The Raven also may be taken as a representative poem of its author, for its exemplification of all his notions of what a poem should be. These are found in his essays on "The Poetic Principle," "The Rationale of Verse," and "The Philosophy of Composition." Poe declared that "in Music, perhaps, the soul most nearly attains the great end for which, when inspired by the Poetic Sentiment, it struggles—the creation of supernal Beauty.... Verse cannot be better designated than as an inferior or less capable music"; but again, verse which is really the "Poetry of Words" is "The Rhythmical Creation of Beauty,"—this and nothing more. The *tone* of the highest Beauty is one of Sadness. The most melancholy of topics is Death. This must be allied to Beauty. "The death, then, of a beautiful woman is, unquestionably, the most poetical topic in the world,—and equally is it beyond doubt that the lips best suited for such a topic are those of a bereaved lover." These last expressions are quoted from Poe's whimsical analysis of this very poem, but they indicate precisely the general range of his verse. The climax of "The Bells" is the muffled monotone of ghouls, who glory in weighing down the human heart. "Lenore," *The Raven*, "The Sleeper," "To One in Paradise," and "Ulalume" form a tenebrose symphony,—and "Annabel Lee," written last of all, shows that one theme possessed him to the end. Again, these are all nothing if not musical, and some are touched with that quality of the Fantastic which awakes the sense of awe, and adds a new fear to agony itself. Through all is dimly outlined, beneath a shadowy pall, the poet's ideal love,—so often half-portrayed elsewhere,—the entombed wife of Usher, the Lady Ligeia, in truth the counterpart of his own nature. I suppose that an artist's love for one "in the form" never can wholly rival his devotion to some ideal. The woman near him must exercise her spells, be all by turns and nothing long, charm him with infinite variety, or be content to forego a share of his allegiance. He must be lured by the Unattainable, and this is ever just beyond him in his passion for creative art.

Poe, like Hawthorne, came in with the decline of the Romantic school, and none delighted more than he to laugh at its calamity. Yet his heart was with the romancers and their Oriental or Gothic effects. His invention, so rich in the prose tales, seemed to desert him when he wrote verse; and his judgment told him that long romantic poems depend more upon incident than inspiration,—and that, to utter the poetry of romance, lyrics would suffice. Hence his theory, clearly fitted to his own limitations, that "a 'long poem' is a flat contradiction in terms." The components of *The Raven* are few and simple: a man, a bird, and the phantasmal memory at a woman. But the piece affords a fine display of romantic material. What have we? The midnight; the shadowy chamber with its tomes of forgotten lore; the student,—a modern Hieronymus; the raven's tap on the casement; the wintry night and dying fire; the silken wind-swept hangings; the dreams and vague mistrust of the echoing darkness; the black, uncanny bird upon the pallid bust; the accessories of violet velvet and the gloating lamp. All this stage effect of situation, light, color, sound, is purely romantic, and even melodramatic, but of a poetic quality that melodrama rarely exhibits, and thoroughly reflective of the poet's "eternal passion, eternal pain."

The rhythmical structure of *The Raven* was sure to make an impression. Rhyme, alliteration, the burden, the stanzaic form, were devised with singular adroitness. Doubtless the poet was struck with the aptness of Miss Barrett's musical trochaics, in "eights," and especially by the arrangement adopted near the close of "Lady Geraldine":

"'Eyes,' he said, 'now throbbing through me! Are ye eyes that did undo me?
Shining eyes, like antique jewels set in Parian statue-stone!
Underneath that calm white forehead, are ye ever burning torrid
O'er the desolate sand-desert of my heart and life undone?'"

His artistic introduction of a third rhyme in both the second and fourth lines, and the addition of a fifth line and a final refrain, made the stanza of *The Raven*. The persistent alliteration seems to come without effort, and often the rhymes within lines are seductive; while the refrain or burden dominates the whole work. Here also he had profited by Miss Barrett's study of ballads and romaunts in her own and other tongues. A "refrain" is the lure wherewith a poet or a musician holds the wandering ear,—the recurrent longing of Nature for the initial strain. I have always admired the beautiful refrains of the English songstress,—"The Nightingales, the Nightingales," "Margret, Margret," "My Heart and I," "Toll slowly," "The River floweth on," "Pan, Pan is dead," etc. She also employed what I term the Repetend, in the use of which Poe has excelled all poets since Coleridge thus revived it:

"O happy living things! no tongue
Their beauty might declare:
A spring of love gushed from my heart,
And I blessed them unaware:
Sure my kind saint took pity on me,
And I blessed them unaware."

Poe created the fifth line of his stanza for the magic of the repetend. He relied upon it to the uttermost in a few later poems,—"Lenore," "Annabel Lee," "Ulalume," and "For Annie." It gained a wild and melancholy music, I have thought, from the "sweet influences," of the Afric burdens and repetends that were sung to him in childhood, attuning with their native melody the voice of our Southern poet.

"The Philosophy of Composition," his analysis of *The Raven*, is a technical dissection of its method and structure. Neither his avowal of cold-blooded artifice, nor his subsequent avowal to friends that an exposure of this artifice was only another of his intellectual hoaxes, need be wholly credited. If he had designed the complete work in advance, he scarcely would have made so harsh a prelude of rattle-pan rhymes to the delicious melody of the second stanza,—not even upon his theory of the fantastic. Of course an artist, having perfected a work, sees, like the first Artist, that it is good, and sees why it is good. A subsequent analysis, coupled with a disavowal of any sacred fire, readily enough may be made. My belief is that the first conception and rough draft of this poem came as inspiration always comes; that its author then saw how it might be perfected, giving it the final touches described in his chapter on Composition, and that the latter, therefore, is neither wholly false nor wholly true. The harm of such analysis is that it tempts a novice to fancy that artificial processes can supersede imagination. The impulse of genius is to guard the secrets of its creative hour. Glimpses obtained of the toil, the baffled experiments, which precede a triumph, as in the sketch-work of Hawthorne recently brought to light, afford priceless instruction and encouragement to the sincere artist. But one who voluntarily exposes his Muse to the gaze of all comers should recall the fate of King Candaules.

The world still thinks of Poe as a "luckless man of genius." I recently heard him mentioned as "one whom everybody seems chartered to misrepresent, decry or slander." But it seems to me that his ill-luck ended with his pitiable death, and that since then his defence has been persistent, and his fame of as steadfast growth as a suffering and gifted author could pray for in his hopeful hour. Griswold's decrial and slander turned the current in his favor. Critics and biographers have come forward with successive refutations, with tributes to his character, with new editions of his works. His own letters and the minute incidents of his career are before us; the record, good and bad, is widely known. No appellor has received more tender and forgiving judgement. His mishaps in life belonged to his region and period, perchance still more to his own infirmity of will. Doubtless his environment was not one to guard a fine-grained, ill-balanced nature from perils without and within. His strongest will, to be lord of himself, gained for him "that heritage of woe." He confessed himself the bird's unhappy master, the stricken sufferer of this poem. But his was a full share of that dramatic temper which exults in the presage of its own doom. There is a delight in playing one's high part: we are all gladiators, crying *Ave Imperator!* To quote Burke's matter of fact: "In grief the pleasure is still uppermost, and the affliction we suffer has no resemblance to absolute pain, which is always odious, and which we endeavor to shake off as soon as possible." Poe went farther, and was an artist even in the tragedy of his career. If, according to his own belief, sadness and the vanishing of beauty are the highest poetic themes, and poetic feeling the keenest earthly pleasure, then the sorrow and darkness of his broken life were not without their frequent compensation.

In the following pages, we have a fresh example of an artist's genius characterizing his interpretation of a famous poem. Gustave Doré, the last work of whose pencil is before us, was not the painter, or even the draughtsman, for realists demanding truth of tone, figure, and perfection. Such matters concerned him less than to make shape and distance, light and shade, assist his purpose,—which was to excite the soul, the imagination, of the looker on. This he did by arousing our sense of awe, through marvellous and often sublime conceptions of things unutterable and full of gloom or glory. It is well said that if his works were not great paintings, as pictures they are great indeed. As a "literary artist," and such he was, his force was in direct ratio with the dramatic invention of his author, with the brave audacities of the spirit that kindled his own. Hence his success with Rabelais, with "Le Juif-Errant," "Les Contes Drolatiques," and "Don Quixote," and hence, conversely, his failure to express the beauty of Tennyson's Idyls, of "Il Paradiso," of the Hebrew pastorals, and other texts requiring exaltation, or sweetness and repose. He was a born master of the grotesque, and by a special insight could portray the spectres of a haunted brain. We see objects as his personages saw them, and with the very eyes of the Wandering Jew, the bewildered Don, or the goldsmith's daughter whose fancy so magnifies the King in the shop on the Pont-au-Change. It was in the nature of things that he should be attracted to each masterpiece of verse or prose that I have termed unique. The lower kingdoms were called into his service; his rocks, trees and mountains, the sky itself, are animate with motive and diablerie. Had he lived to illustrate Shakespeare, we should have seen a remarkable treatment of Caliban, the Witches, the storm in "Lear"; but doubtless should have questioned his ideals of Imogen or Miranda. Beauty pure and simple, and the perfect excellence thereof, he rarely seemed to comprehend.

Yet there is beauty in his designs for the "Ancient Mariner," unreal as they are, and a consecutiveness rare in a series by Doré. The Rime afforded him a prolonged story, with many shiftings of the scene. In *The Raven* sound and color preserve their monotone and we have no change of place or occasion. What is the result? Doré proffers a series of variations upon the theme as he conceived it, "the enigma of death and the hallucination of an inconsolable soul." In some of these drawings his faults are evident; others reveal his powerful originality, and the best qualities in which, as a draughtsman, he stood alone. Plainly there was something in common between the working moods of Poe and Doré. This would appear more clearly had the latter tried his hand upon the "Tales of the Grotesque and Arabesque." Both resorted often to the elf-land of fantasy and romance. In melodramatic feats they both, through their command of the supernatural, avoided the danger-line between the ideal and the absurd. Poe was the truer worshipper of the Beautiful; his love for it was a consecrating passion, and herein he parts company with his illustrator. Poet or artist, Death at last transfigures all: within the shadow of his sable harbinger, Vedder's symbolic crayon aptly sets them face to face, but enfolds them with the mantle of immortal wisdom and power. An American woman has wrought the image of a star-eyed Genius with the final torch, the exquisite semblance of one whose vision beholds, but whose lips may not utter, the mysteries of a land beyond "the door of a legended tomb."

Edmund C. Stedman.

THE POEM

THE RAVEN

Once upon a midnight dreary, while I pondered, weak and weary,
Over many a quaint and curious volume of forgotten lore,
While I nodded, nearly napping, suddenly there came a tapping,
As of some one gently rapping, rapping at my chamber door.
"'T is some visiter," I muttered, "tapping at my chamber door—
Only this, and nothing more."
Ah, distinctly I remember it was in the bleak December,
And each separate dying ember wrought its ghost upon the floor.
Eagerly I wished the morrow:—vainly I had sought to borrow
From my books surcease of sorrow—sorrow for the lost Lenore—
For the rare and radiant maiden whom the angels name Lenore—
Nameless here for evermore.
And the silken sad uncertain rustling of each purple curtain
Thrilled me—filled me with fantastic terrors never felt before;
So that now, to still the beating of my heart, I stood repeating
"'T is some visiter entreating entrance at my chamber door
Some late visiter entreating entrance at my chamber door;—
This it is, and nothing more."
Presently my soul grew stronger; hesitating then no longer,
"Sir," said I, "or Madam, truly your forgiveness I implore;
But the fact is I was napping, and so gently you came rapping,
And so faintly you came tapping, tapping at my chamber door,
That I scarce was sure I heard you"—here I opened wide the door;—
Darkness there, and nothing more.
Deep into that darkness peering, long I stood there wondering, fearing,
Doubting, dreaming dreams no mortal ever dared to dream before;
But the silence was unbroken, and the darkness gave no token,
And the only word there spoken was the whispered word, "Lenore!"
This I whispered, and an echo murmured back the word, "Lenore!"
Merely this and nothing more.
Back into the chamber turning, all my soul within me burning,
Soon again I heard a tapping, somewhat louder than before.
"Surely," said I, "surely that is something at my window lattice;
Let me see, then, what thereat is, and this mystery explore—

Let my heart be still a moment and this mystery explore;—
'T is the wind and nothing more!"
Open here I flung the shutter, when, with many a flirt and flutter,
In there stepped a stately Raven of the saintly days of yore.
Not the least obeisance made he; not a minute stopped or stayed he;
But, with mien of lord or lady, perched above my chamber door—
Perched upon a bust of Pallas just above my chamber door—
Perched, and sat, and nothing more.
Then this ebony bird beguiling my sad fancy into smiling,
By the grave and stern decorum of the countenance it wore,
"Though thy crest be shorn and shaven, thou," I said, "art sure no
craven,
Ghastly grim and ancient Raven wandering from the Nightly shore,—
Tell me what thy lordly name is on the Night's Plutonian shore!"
Quoth the Raven, "Nevermore."
Much I marvelled this ungainly fowl to hear discourse so plainly,
Though its answer little meaning—little relevancy bore;
For we cannot help agreeing that no living human being
Ever yet was blessed with seeing bird above his chamber door—
Bird or beast upon the sculptured bust above his chamber door,
With such name as "Nevermore."
But the Raven, sitting lonely on the placid bust, spoke only
That one word, as if his soul in that one word he did outpour.
Nothing further then he uttered—not a feather then he fluttered—
Till I scarcely more than muttered, "Other friends have flown
before—
On the morrow *he* will leave me, as my hopes have flown before."
Then the bird said, "Nevermore."
Startled at the stillness broken by reply so aptly spoken,
"Doubtless," said I, "what it utters is its only stock and store,
Caught from some unhappy master whom unmerciful Disaster
Followed fast and followed faster till his songs one burden bore—
Till the dirges of his Hope that melancholy burden bore
Of 'Never—nevermore.'"
But the Raven still beguiling all my sad soul into smiling,
Straight I wheeled a cushioned seat in front of bird and bust and door;
Then, upon the velvet sinking, I betook myself to linking

Fancy unto fancy, thinking what this ominous bird of yore—
What this grim, ungainly, ghastly, gaunt and ominous bird of yore
Meant in croaking "Nevermore."
This I sat engaged in guessing, but no syllable expressing
To the fowl whose fiery eyes now burned into my bosom's core;
This and more I sat divining, with my head at ease reclining
On the cushion's velvet lining that the lamplight gloated o'er,
But whose velvet violet lining with the lamplight gloating o'er
She shall press, ah, nevermore!
Then, methought, the air grew denser, perfumed from an unseen
censer
Swung by seraphim whose foot-falls tinkled on the tufted floor.
"Wretch," I cried, "thy God hath lent thee—by these angels he hath
sent thee
Respite—respite and nepenthe from thy memories of Lenore!
Quaff, oh quaff this kind nepenthe, and forget this lost Lenore!"
Quoth the Raven, "Nevermore."
"Prophet!" said I, "thing of evil!—prophet still, if bird or devil!—
Whether Tempter sent, or whether tempest tossed thee here ashore,
Desolate yet all undaunted, on this desert land enchanted—
On this home by Horror haunted—tell me truly, I implore—
Is there—*is* there balm in Gilead?—tell me—tell me, I implore!"
Quoth the Raven, "Nevermore."
"Prophet!" said I, "thing of evil—prophet still, if bird or devil!
By that Heaven that bends above, us—by that God we both adore—
Tell this soul with sorrow laden if, within the distant Aidenn,
It shall clasp a sainted maiden whom the angels name Lenore—
Clasp a rare and radiant maiden whom the angels name Lenore."
Quoth the Raven, "Nevermore."
"Be that word our sign of parting, bird or fiend!" I shrieked,
upstarting—
"Get thee back into the tempest and the Night's Plutonian shore!
Leave no black plume as a token of that lie thy soul hath spoken!
Leave my loneliness unbroken!—quit the bust above my door!
Take thy beak from out my heart, and take thy form from off my
door!"
Quoth the Raven, "Nevermore."

And the Raven, never flitting, still is sitting, still is sitting
On the pallid bust of Pallas just above my chamber door;
And his eyes have all the seeming of a demon's that is dreaming,
And the lamplight o'er him streaming throws his shadow on the floor;
And my soul from out that shadow that lies floating on the floor
Shall be lifted—nevermore!

"Once upon a midnight dreary, while I pondered, weak and weary,
Over many a quaint and curious volume of forgotten lore."

"Ah, distinctly I remember it was in the bleak December,
And each separate dying ember wrought its ghost upon the floor."

"Eagerly I wished the morrow;—vainly I had sought to borrow
From my books surcease of sorrow—sorrow for the lost Lenore."

"Sorrow for the lost Lenore."

"For the rare and radiant maiden whom the angels name Lenore—
Nameless here for evermore."

"'T is some visiter entreating entrance at my chamber door—
Some late visiter entreating entrance at my chamber door.'"

"Here I opened wide the door;—
Darkness there, and nothing more."

"Doubting, dreaming dreams no mortal ever dared to dream before."

"'Surely,' said I, 'surely that is something at my window lattice;
Let me see, then, what thereat is, and this mystery explore.'"

"Open here I flung the shutter."

. . . . "A stately Raven of the saintly days of yore.
Not the least obeisance made he; not a minute stopped or stayed he."

"Perched upon a bust of Pallas just above my chamber door—
Perched, and sat, and nothing more."

"Wandering from the Nightly shore."

"Till I scarcely more than muttered, 'Other friends have flown
before—
On the morrow *he* will leave me, as my hopes have flown before.'"

"Then, upon the velvet sinking, I betook myself to linking
Fancy unto fancy."

"But whose velvet violet lining with the lamplight gloating o'er
She shall press, ah, nevermore!"

"'Wretch,' I cried, 'thy God hath lent thee—by these angels he hath
sent thee
Respite—respite and nepenthe from thy memories of Lenore!'"

"On this home by Horror haunted."

. . . . "Tell me truly, I implore—
Is there—*is* there balm in Gilead?—tell me—tell me, I implore!"

"Tell this soul with sorrow laden if, within the distant Aidenn,
It shall clasp a sainted maiden whom the angels name Lenore."

"'Be that word our sign of parting, bird or fiend!' I shrieked, upstarting."

"'Get thee back into the tempest and the Night's Plutonian shore!'"

"And my soul from out that shadow that lies floating on the floor
Shall be lifted—nevermore!"

Made in the USA
Coppell, TX
24 May 2020

26390544R00028